UNUSUAL OBJECTS IN FANTASTIC PLACES

To Steven Spielberg, whose amazing movies
have inspired us since our childhood

Also by Mark Penta & T.M. Murphy

Super Strange Story Starters

Creative Coloring and Far-Out Fun

TOTALLY WEIRD ACTIVITY BOOKS

UNUSUAL OBJECTS IN FANTASTIC PLACES

A STORY STARTER BOOK

Created by illustrator Mark Penta & writer T.M. Murphy

WEST
MARGIN
PRESS

West Margin Press
An imprint of Turner Publishing Company
Nashville, Tennessee
www.turnerpublishing.com

WEST
MARGIN
PRESS

Library of Congress Control Number: 2023930545

Printed in the United States of America

UNUSUAL OBJECTS IN FANTASTIC PLACES

HOW TO USE THIS BOOK

This book is full of super strange stories for you to read. Each story ends with a cliff-hanger. Your job is to imagine what happens next! All you need is something to write with. You can use the blank lines to finish your favorite story starters. If you need more space to write, there are more blank lines in the back of the book. If you want, you can even draw additional characters or scenes!

Are you ready to read and write some totally weird stories?

Then turn the page and have fun!

THE TIME MACHINE IN DINOSAUR VALLEY

The year was 2424, and Ronin Hebert wanted to get an A in history class, so she thought she'd spend the weekend doing an assignment. Ronin went into the attic and jumped into her grandfather's time machine. She set a course for 80 million years ago.

The machine rocketed through the past before stopping at the Cretaceous era. The door swooshed open, and Ronin stepped out. She dove to the side, barely avoiding a T. Rex's foot. It continued in hot pursuit of a Triceratops.

"Wow, gotta be careful," she said, wiping herself off. For the next ten minutes, she shot videos and collected rock samples. Her plan was to return home and write up the assignment. Pretty simple.

It all changed when she spotted a woman in rags sneaking into the time machine.

"No!" Ronin yelled, sprinting, and raising her fist to pound on the door, but the machine disappeared into thin air.

It makes no sense, she thought. *People weren't alive during this time period. Did I land in an alternate world, or was that woman from 2424?*

Over the mountaintop, a red flare suddenly streaked through the sky.

Oh, thank goodness, I'm not alone.

She took her first step in the direction of the flare when . . .

_____

_____

_____

_____

_____

_____

_____

Continued on page _____

THE ICE CREAM TRUCK AT FORTUNE FOUNTAIN

The group of kids could hardly believe it when an ice cream truck appeared at Fortune Fountain. Everyone except for Chris and Jo raced to get in line.

After waiting on the last customer, the driver looked over at them. "You next?"

Chris shrugged. "No money."

"Then you get something special," she smiled, digging into the freezer before handing them each a popsicle.

"Why give us free popsicles?" Chris asked.

"You'll see." She winked.

With that, the truck lifted two feet off the ground, a pink cloud billowed from the exhaust pipe, and poof – it disappeared.

"Whoa," they exclaimed. They sat and enjoyed their popsicles until only the sticks remained.

"Chris, look!" Jo shouted. Written in tiny lettering on the sticks was a message:

Swirl this in the fountain
Wish for anyone but you
That's the sweetest way
To make your dreams come true

They sprinted to the fountain, dipped the sticks in, and made their wishes. The water began to churn and...

_____

_____

_____

Continued on page _____

THE GONDOLIER'S HAT IN THE GRAND CANAL

It's an incredible honor to be a gondolier in Venice, Italy, but Mattia Giovanni didn't care. He had stopped pursuing his dream of becoming an opera singer to join the family business of rowing gondolas in the Grand Canal. He rarely sang anymore, but today a sudden urge came over him. While steering the gondola for a cuddling honeymoon couple, he began to sing. A moment later, his hat blew away. Frustrated and embarrassed, he stopped singing.

What's the point? he thought.

He reached down to retrieve his hat just as a pink dolphin popped its head up and out of the water. It was wearing his hat. The dolphin moved excitedly from side to side.

"I think he wants an encore and so do we," said the new bride.

With that, the dolphin leaped in the air and the hat landed back on Mattia's head.

People cheered and pointed from the windows of the buildings that were lined along the banks. Mattia smiled widely, realizing he had a captive audience. That's when . . .

_____

_____

_____

_____

_____

_____

_____

_____

_____

_____

_____

Continued on page _____

THE TRUNK AT BOBSLED SKATE PARK

Vicki was much older than her twelve-year-old stepsister Beth, but they both had something in common. They loved to skateboard. Wearing helmets, knee pads, and carrying their boards, the stepsisters walked through the woods together.

"I don't get it. How are we going to go skateboarding out here?" Beth asked.

"You'll see. Just a little longer," Vicki responded, and after ten minutes Beth understood. "It looks like a dead cement monster. What is it?" Beth asked.

"It's an abandoned bobsled track from the Winter Olympics, but today it's our skate park." Vicki sprinted toward the track and Beth followed.

Vicki took the lead as their boards hugged the cement. They quickly picked up speed—too much speed!

Vicki headed straight for the vandalized section. Rock and debris blocked her path. She gave a warning wave to Beth before gliding around it.

But she was forced to ride the curved track up and into the air. She came crashing down onto something.

That was stupid! Vicki thought. *I should've inspected the track first. I'm lucky to be alive.*

Vicki got up and saw that she had landed on an old trunk. There were initials on it: MMP. She pressed the latch and the trunk popped open. She looked inside and . . .

_____

_____

_____

_____

_____

_____

Continued on page _____

THE RAVEN DRONE AT BRICKFORD MILL

Szal Diamond Company secretly purchased the Brickford Mill because of the massive sixty-foot brick wall that enclosed it. They didn't want anyone to know they were renovating it into a diamond cutting facility since it could attract thieves.

No one in town knew that secret, including twelve-year-old Andre Dixon. He was up the street playing with his raven drone when he first spotted flames rising in the distance.

"The mill's on fire! I gotta check this out," he said to himself while staring through his goggles and guiding his handheld motion controller.

A moment later, the raven drone buzzed over the high walls and Andre could view the chaos below. Workers evacuated the building as flames exploded windows. Some people carried black suitcases as they ran for the gates, but Andre focused in on a man who stopped and hurled something that landed on the top of the wall.

Andre moved the controller and the raven drone descended for a closer look. That's when his jaw dropped. It was a blue diamond the size of a golf ball. His next decision would change his life forever. Andre decided to . . .

_____

_____

_____

_____

_____

_____

_____

_____

_____

Continued on page _____

THE GREEK GODS' REVENGE AT ACROPOLIS ARCADE

One minute, Nikki Lowen was nearing the high score on the video arcade game *Greek Gods' Revenge*, and the next, she was climbing the steps of the Parthenon. The game suddenly slammed on the ground beside her. She looked around and saw a dozen kids feverishly moving controllers to their own games.

"How'd I get here?" she wondered out loud.

A boy came forward. "By being rude to Ms. Baros," he said.

"My substitute teacher?" Nikki was confused because he was right. Ms. Baros had taken her phone away in history class earlier that day. Nikki had caused a scene when she blurted out, "You're not even a real teacher!"

The boy brought her back to the moment. "Ms. Baros hates when students disrupt her lesson on ancient Greece. In 1982, I was shooting spitballs and was sent to the office. That night, I went to the arcade and boom, I ended up here."

"1982? But it's 2024 and you're my age."

"We don't age here. You're one of many she has sent. You just made it harder for all of us."

"Harder?"

"To get back you need to get the high score on each arcade game. What's yours called?"

"Greek Gods' Revenge."

"Seriously?! We must find shelter. It's almost sundown. That's when the games come alive." he said.

A lightning bolt shot from the sky and . . .

_____

_____

_____

Continued on page _____

THE TOUR BUS AT PALM TREE STADIUM

The Levitating Frogs band formed when all four members met at a summer school science class. Tag played guitar, Arnie played bass, and Stretch was on drums. Jimbo couldn't play a lick, but he had charisma and declared himself their lead singer. He also named the band in memory of the frogs they dissected in class.

They'd had some success over the years, but now they couldn't even afford a driver. Jimbo was driving their tour bus through a blinding snowstorm, thinking that it was probably time for the band to call it quits.

If we could just do one more gig, he thought as the wipers cleared away the snowflakes. The bus's headlights illuminated a sign that read *Next Exit: Palm Tree Stadium.*

That's a weird name, Jimbo thought, considering he was driving in Vermont. Since the rest of the band was asleep, he decided to take the exit. When he pulled off the highway, the snow turned into a sandstorm.

What the heck is going on, he wondered. The bus plowed ahead. Sunlight blinded him before he slammed to a stop.

Arnie shouted, "Dudes, we're on an island!"

Tag pointed at the sea. "Look."

Hundreds of boats were headed their way.

Five minutes later . . .

_____

_____

_____

_____

_____

_____

Continued on page _____

THE BIKE IN THE MYSTERIOUS DESERT

I don't know who I am.

It was a mystery to her. She guessed that she was in her early twenties. But who was she and how did she end up in the middle of a desert? She searched for a wallet or an ID in her pockets but there wasn't any. She did have a couple of clues, though. She was carrying rock climbing gear, and there was a mountain in the distance.

Was I rock climbing? Did I fall and hit my head?

She felt her head for injuries. Nothing.

Usually, people don't go climbing alone. There must be someone out here who knows me.

There was no one in sight. Fear gripped her when she realized that she didn't have any water.

I have to get moving before the desert sun takes my energy.

She lumbered on for what felt like hours, and then she saw it—a rusty child's bike resting against a cactus. It had a personalized license plate attached to the back of the seat. It read: *Amelia.*

Who is Amelia, and why is her bike here?

The bike was too small for her, but she didn't have any other choice. She sat on it, pedaling furiously, hoping all her questions would be answered soon, when suddenly . . .

_____

_____

_____

_____

_____

Continued on page _____

THE HERO'S MASK AT FEAR POINT CITY

The residents of Fear Point City didn't know Tej's real identity. They didn't even know Tej's gender, and they didn't care. All they cared about was that the masked, martial arts superhero flew around cleaning up the streets.

Mayor Molloy even proposed it was time to change the name of the city since all fear had been erased. At least, that's what everyone thought!

Tej was taking a day off from crime fighting to do laundry when the frantic call came.

"Tej!" Mayor Molloy screamed into the phone. "There's someone wearing a jet pack like yours, but it's a different color. It's red. The villain is threatening to burn down city hall unless you come here now!"

There was no time to think. Tej grabbed the jet pack and blasted into the sky before realizing the mask was still on the line.

Tej pushed the landing switch and headed back down.

Oh, no!

Tej spotted a little girl pulling the mask off the line.

Don't put it on! Tej's mind screamed. It was too late. The girl put the mask on and . . .

_____

_____

_____

_____

_____

_____

_____

_____

Continued on page _____

THE PIRATE SHIP AT ATLANTIS TOY STORE

Cameron Woods sat in the library with his face buried in a book about underwater mysteries. His dream was to sail around the world. Many thought it was a silly fantasy considering Cameron lived in Nebraska.

"You won't believe what I just heard!" His friend Josh jumped into the chair next to him.

"What?"

"Sophie bought roller skates at that weird new toy store. You know, the one owned by the woman with the green seaweed hair. She claims her skates have magical powers, and she rolled to Ohio in ten minutes."

Cameron laughed at the outrageous lie, but that afternoon he walked into the toy store. The toys were as ancient as the woman behind the counter who smiled at him.

"You're the boy who wants to swim around the world."

"How did you know that?" Cameron asked, surprised.

"See that toy pirate ship? Grab it and meet me in the alley."

Moments later, the woman appeared carrying a large bucket of water. "Drop the ship in the bucket."

He did, and suddenly, the bucket overflowed. Water began flooding the alley, as the toy grew into an enormous pirate ship. A real pirate loomed over the bow and hollered, "Mate, if you want the adventure, you'll have to jump in and swim to me!"

Cameron eyed the safety of the sidewalk and the raging, ocean alley. He took a deep breath and . . .

_____

_____

_____

Continued on page _____

THE JOURNAL AT THE TROPICAL HIDEAWAY

Thirteen-year-old Harmony Sinclair had been raised in the jungle. Her parents bought the Tropical Hideaway Resort when she was just an infant. Their goal was to run a profitable business while teaching Harmony to appreciate nature.

The Sinclairs had succeeded in both areas, but Harmony was becoming restless with the quiet lifestyle. Feeling bored, she began her daily chore of placing books on the shelves of the outdoor lending library.

When the books were in order, Harmony's pet snake, Bookmark, appeared and slithered around.

"You just can't help yourself," Harmony said and smiled. The first day they met, Bookmark had been sunning himself on the outdoor bookcase.

Harmony came out of her memory when she noticed a red book with the word *Journal* on it.

That's weird! That wasn't here a minute ago.

Curious, she slowly opened it. The first entry was dated 1949. It read, *"If you are reading this, you need to know the secrets of the jungle. It all begins with . . .*

_____

_____

_____

_____

_____

_____

_____

_____

Continued on page _____

THE GUMBALL MACHINE AT THE PYRAMIDS OF GIZA

When the giant gumball machine first appeared in front of the ancient pyramids of Giza, tour guide Omar Ali thought it was probably the work of some trendy artist trying to make people talk. But no one took credit for it, so Omar wondered if Cleopatra's Candy Shop put it there to cash in on the tourist dollars. His theory didn't make sense since the machine only took American quarters, and even the tourists used Egyptian currency.

Omar then realized something strange. He was the only person who noticed the machine. Tourists and other employees walked past it without saying a word.

Omar mentioned it to a co-worker who laughed and suggested the desert heat was playing tricks with his mind.

This frightened Omar, so the next day he brought a quarter that he had saved from his trip to the States. He put it in the machine, turned the lever, and . . .

Continued on page _____

31

THE HAND OF FORGIVENESS BRIDGE

When Jodi Freeman got the call to be on a game show in Los Angeles, saying that all her expenses would be paid for, she jumped at the chance. When it happened to Melanie Salter, she also didn't blink an eye. Now both were on opposite ends of a bridge, nervously following the director's instructions to walk up and over it. They both wondered why the bridge was underneath a large statue of a hand.

The cameraperson zoomed in on the host, who stood below the bridge. He spoke in a dramatic whisper that grew. "Jodi and Melanie know they are on a game show, but they don't know what's about to happen. You see, tonight's contestants on *Forgiveness Bridge* got into a fight four years ago. They vowed never to speak to one another ever again and haven't seen each other since. In ten seconds, that will change. If they want to win tonight's big mystery prize, they'll have to resolve their differences!"

At that point, the game show music began playing, and the fingers of the hand slowly moved. "When the hand fully closes, your time is up. Now, try to get over your differences. Good luck," the game show host said.

Jodi and Melanie were in shock as their eyes locked on one another. They couldn't believe it. Jodi was the first to speak. She said, ". . .

_____

_____

_____

_____

_____

_____

_____

_____

Continued on page _____

THE FERRIS WHEEL AT CRANE'S CARNIVAL

Carnival worker Jared Rose eyed the elderly man.

"We're about to close. Do you really think you should go on this ride? You seem a bit . . . old."

"In 1943, they said I was too short and now I'm too old. Let me pass. It's been a great visit." The man swatted his cane, shooing Jared aside. Settled in his passenger car, the old man handed the cane over.

"This protected me. I don't need it now. It will save your life."

Jared laughed and grabbed the cane. He walked over to pull the lever.

Only one customer and I still have to run the ride, Jared thought.

While the music droned on, he stared up at the sky. He then realized he wasn't staring at stars. They were fast-moving lights headed for the carnival. The Ferris wheel grinded to a halt.

Oh no!

Jared yanked the lever up and down. The wheel restarted, but now it spun dangerously fast. The old man cackled with glee as Jared watched in horror. The wheel snapped off its holder, dropped in mid-air to its side, and transformed into a flying saucer. It hovered for a moment before shooting off and joining the other moving lights, instantly vanishing into the night sky.

Was that real?

On the ground, glowing like the color of the alien lights, was the cane. Jared picked it up and . . .

_____

_____

_____

Continued on page _____

THE GIFT AT CUPCAKE FARMS

Cupcake Farms was one of the best venues to host birthday parties and events. It wasn't just because of the world-famous cupcakes. The main attraction was Miss Majestic, the only horse known to have a purple-colored mane. People traveled from all over just to get a picture with her.

On this day, a boy's fourteenth birthday party was being held when Miss Majestic spotted a teenage girl with purple hair walking towards her. Miss Majestic had never seen such beautiful hair on a person before, so she whinnied with happiness.

"This is a private party," the birthday boy snapped at the girl. "No purple haired weirdos allowed."

His six friends laughed while eating their cupcakes. Miss Majestic didn't understand the boy's words, but she knew he was being mean.

The girl ignored the comment and said, "Hello Miss Majestic. I've come a long way to give you this special gift as a thank you for inspiring me to be my true self."

Miss Majestic watched as the girl slowly unwrapped a box. The boys couldn't understand why she would give that kind of gift to a horse. But Miss Majestic knew the reason.

She galloped toward the fence, leaped over it, and . . .

_____

_____

_____

_____

_____

_____

_____

_____

_____

_____

_____

Continued on page _____

THE POSTCARDS AT TORNADO ALLEY

Most boys living in the Texas Panhandle wanted to be cowboys, but twelve-year-old Wes Cady wanted to write about them. His dream was to become a famous Western writer, so he carried a notebook everywhere.

Unfortunately, his family lived in Tornado Alley where twisters came from out of nowhere. That's exactly what happened to Wes while he walked to school one day. He dropped his notebook, raced for shelter, and watched his stories blow into the sky. A week later, Wes was feeding his horse when another tornado hit, this time depositing debris onto the stable. After the twister passed, Wes noticed several postcards scattered on the ground.

They were all addressed to him!

He began reading one: "I loved your story, *Kid Cattle Rancher*. Please send us more."

Us? he wondered, and picked up another: "Mr. Cady, you are my favorite writer."

All of the postcards were about his stories and dated 1892. There were two postcards left.

He read the first one: "We at Cowboy Cady's Fan Club have sent you a blank card hoping you can write a story about Dead Tree Hill. Please throw it into the next twister."

Sure enough, the next postcard was blank and bigger than the rest. Wes sprinted to his house. He opened the laptop and searched for "Dead Tree Hill 1892."

He couldn't believe what he found. He had to warn them. Thunder boomed in the distance. A new twister was coming. He furiously wrote on the card: "Dear People of Dead Tree Hill . . .

_____

_____

_____

Continued on page _____

THE ENVELOPE AT SILVERTON MANSION

An estate sale is when all the items inside someone's house are available for purchase. They usually occur when the owner of the house has died.

Tonya Ross learned that definition from her grandfather when she was nine years old. It was now their monthly routine to shop at these old homes. Tonya was fascinated to learn the history of the people and their objects while her grandfather haggled to buy merchandise for his consignment store.

"Papa, who owned this place?" she asked as he parked his truck in front of a mansion.

"Janice Silverton. The story is she worked for a museum in the late 1970s when several paintings were stolen. She lost her job, and the paintings were never recovered. Many think she was behind it, especially after she bought this mansion. How else was she able to afford it?"

Tonya was beyond intrigued while they toured the house, but then Papa Ross's eyes lit up when he heard that gardening equipment was for sale in the garage. While he went off to study some hedge clippers, Tonya spotted an antique table tucked away in the back of the living room.

This would be perfect for my bedroom!

When she tried to move it, she felt something attached under the table. She pulled it off. It was an envelope. She thought it might be the price of the table, so she opened it, but it was . . .

_____

_____

_____

_____

Continued on page _____

41

BENNY THE BEAR OVER THE BERMUDA TRIANGLE

The Bermuda Triangle has a bizarre history of planes and boats that have gone missing.

Captain Suong Pham had been flying the Florida-to-Bermuda route for two years, and she'd never had a problem until today.

The flight attendant had just informed her that a stuffed animal was tied to the wing of the plane.

"It wasn't there when we left Miami," Suong said as she kept her eyes on the skies ahead.

"So, what should we tell the passengers? They're nervous. We *are* flying through the Triangle."

Suong grabbed the microphone. "Hello, everyone, no need to be alarmed about our fuzzy passenger outside. I just hope he brought his passport."

After landing, she came up with a story that the grounds crew had played a prank. Some of the passengers laughed while others pulled out their phones to call and complain.

"She's wrong," a little girl said to her mom as they walked past Suong. "The bear appeared during the flight."

When Suong went outside, a worker cut the bear loose and handed it to her.

She read the luggage tag around its ankle: *Benny is property of the* Ocean Angel.

She couldn't believe it. The *Ocean Angel* was a sailboat that vanished back in 1999. Then things got weirder when . . .

_____

_____

_____

Continued on page _____

THE BOOM BOX ON THE MOON

The year was 2064 and space travel from earth to the moon was as common as riding a bike to a friend's house. What wasn't common was finding an unusual machine from the 1980s floating in a crater on the lunar surface.

But that's exactly what thirteen-year-old twin brothers Peter and Johnny Chang had just found. Of course, they had no idea what they were looking at, so they brought it home and showed their father.

"There is no way you found this there," their father said.

"We did, Dad. Why?" the brothers asked in unison.

"Well, when your great-grandfather was your age, this was known as a boom box."

"What?" they both questioned.

"It's a shame they don't teach pop culture anymore. Anyway, this machine played cassette tapes. People could record music or themselves talking on them. Boom boxes weren't used in space back then, so why would one be there?" their father wondered out loud.

"Look, Dad, there's actually a cassette in it. I wonder what's on it," Peter said.

"There is only one way to find out." He pressed play and heard . . .

_____

_____

_____

_____

_____

_____

_____

_____

_____

_____

Continued on page _____

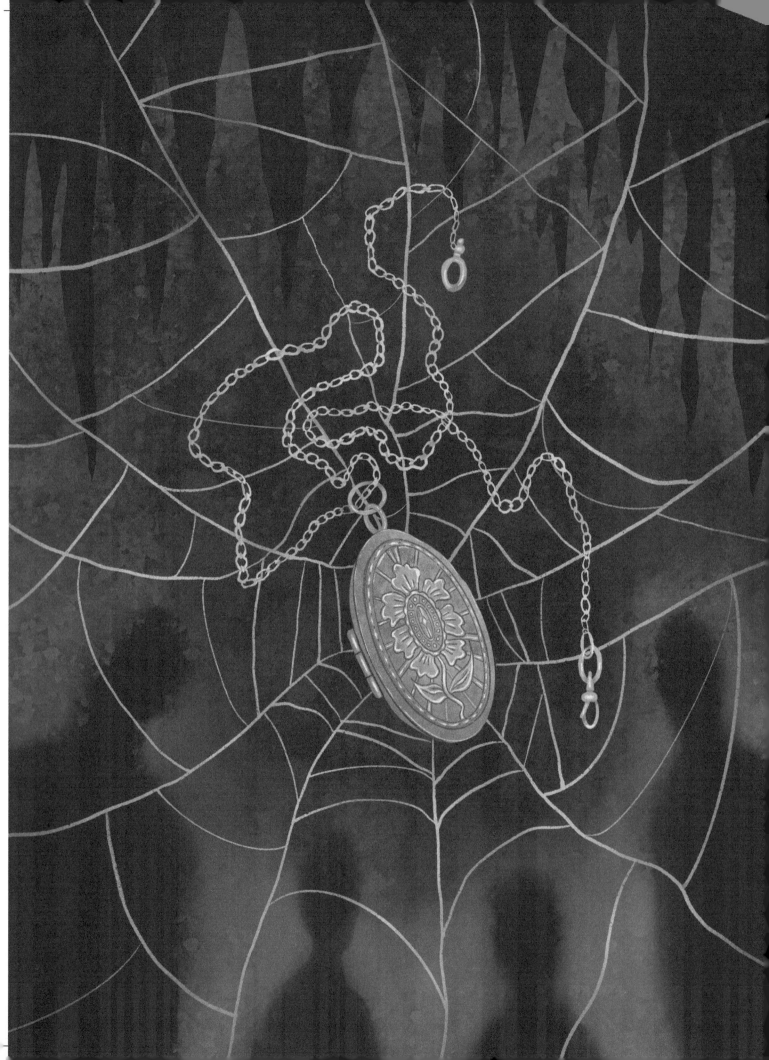

THE GOLD LOCKET AT SPIDERWEB CAVE

Spiderweb Cave was rumored to be a mystical place where strange things often occurred. Brianna Travis had been a park ranger at the cave for three years and loved her job. Other than the thousands of spiderwebs that hung throughout, it was easy to navigate.

Today, she was leading a group of school kids on a tour when they spotted an object hanging from a web. It was a gold locket, but Brianna instantly knew it wasn't just any locket.

"Ranger Travis, I didn't know spiderwebs were strong enough to hold jewelry," one of the kids said.

Brianna seemed mesmerized as she walked toward the web.

"I wonder whose locket it is?" another kid asked.

Brianna carefully took the locket off the web.

She studied it before answering, "It was my grandmother's."

"Your grandmother's? But how did it get in here?" the kid asked.

"I don't know."

Suddenly, a voice from the darkness said, "But I do."

A figure came forward and . . .

_____

_____

_____

_____

_____

_____

_____

Continued on page _____

THE FACELESS MAN OF FRIGID REEF

Nia Jefferson's underwater flashlight illuminated the shadowy figure in the distance. Her eyes instantly bulged at the sight—a man buried to his waist on the bottom of the ocean floor.

Frigid Reef's water was known for preserving artifacts from sunken ships, but this was an unusual find.

Nia kicked her legs, glided closer, and shined the white light on the faceless man before grinning. She realized it was a mannequin dressed in a tuxedo.

Where did this come from, and how did it get here? I should bring this thing up to the boat and prank the crew.

She wrapped her right arm around the mannequin, but then stopped when she spotted a red light heading straight for her. Nia's eyes had every reason to bulge when she realized . . .

_____

_____

_____

_____

_____

_____

_____

_____

_____

_____

_____

Continued on page _____

DRAGON PAINTING AT THE PERFECT CANVAS

Camille Green bused tables at the Perfect Canvas restaurant for one reason—she wanted to meet legendary artists. They all flocked there for the gourmet food, and to use the private studio on the second floor.

Since she was not allowed up there, the eighteen-year-old artist could only imagine why it was considered the best studio in the city.

But on this night, Camille thought maybe she could get an answer. She was clearing a table when she spotted her favorite artist, Gloria Hurst.

Camille walked over. "Ms. Hurst, sorry to bother you, but . . ."

"You want to be an artist like me. But what do you want from your paintings?"

"I want my subjects to jump off the canvas and impact my viewers."

Ms. Hurst handed Camille a key. "I've begun a painting upstairs. Go now and finish it!"

Moments later, Camille stood in the empty studio with a half-painted dragon staring back at her. She moved her brush along the canvas. With each stroke, the room shook. A sharp tail crashed through the back wall that now resembled bricks from a castle.

"How will you paint your way out of this mess?" Ms. Hurst laughed behind her.

As flames burst from the dragon's mouth, Camille took her paintbrush and . . .

_____

_____

_____

_____

_____

_____

_____

Continued on page _____

READY FOR A CREATIVE CHALLENGE?

See the picture on the left? Use the lines below to write a story about it!

What does the message in the bottle say? And why is it floating near a volcanic shore?

_____

_____

_____

_____

_____

_____

_____

_____

_____

_____

_____

_____

_____

_____

_____

_____

_____

_____

_____

Continued on page _____

Read the story on the right, then use the space below to draw a picture of the unusual objects and fantastic place described in the story!

THE BEACH BALL AT TURTLE POND

It had been two months since the basketball team's plane crashed on a deserted island. All twelve passengers of the Jumping Leopards survived, but not one basketball did, which made life boring for the team.

The youngest survivor, eleven-year-old Meekel Washington, smiled and talked to the turtles while washing his clothes in the pond near their camp. He had learned several survival methods from his teammates and was grateful they were alive. They were more than a famous traveling exhibition basketball team to him; they were family. It had also been a valuable time to bond with his dad, the coach, who had always been on the road.

Meekel wished he could do something special for them, and that's when he noticed the ball. He was excited, assuming it was one of the basketballs that got lost in the crash.

"The guys are going to love this!" Meekel exclaimed. He walked toward it, but then he realized something. It wasn't a basketball—it was a beach ball.

What is a beach ball doing here?

He got his answer when he looked up and . . .

_____

_____

_____

_____

_____

_____

_____

_____

Continued on page _____

How to Create Your Own Story Starters!

Part 1

1 Get some supplies! (whichever you prefer!)

Something to write or draw with — Pencils, pens, eraser

a notebook and/or sketchbook — Lined or blank pages

or a computer or tablet — a stylus pen

2 Observe the world around you! Story Starters are made by combining...

people

places

things

Hey! Don't forget us animals, insects and marine life!

psst! write about me!

When you see all this cool stuff, make notes and doodles so you'll remember them later!

How to Create Your Own Story Starters!

Part 2

3 Develop your characters by asking yourself questions about them.

- How do they dress?
- What's their favorite hobby?
- Are they happy, sad, mad?

- What are their dreams?
- What do they say?
- What's their job?
- What's their backstory?

4 ASK: "How can I make this character TOTALLY ORIGINAL?"

Here's the secret:

Look in your notes at your collection of people, places, and things. __Combine__ the most unlikely choices to create a totally unique character and story!

EXAMPLE:

Chef — PERSON

ON the MOON — PLACE

plays a TUBA — THING

owns a NICE HORSE. — ANIMAL?

5) Make ordinary ideas <u>extraordinary</u> by asking "WHAT IF?"

Yo!

what if a scientist invents a talking hot dog?

What if there's buried treasure under the tree?

What if a horse wins the lottery?

Asking "What if" sparks your imagination and helps you think of fun story possibilities!

6) Find a partner to collaborate with!

One can draw a character or scene

the other can write the story

Share your idea with your partner. Maybe a drawing is made first, or maybe the story. It doesn't matter. You don't have to be a super-great artist or writer. The goal is to have fun inspiring each other to create something!

ABOUT THE AUTHORS

T.M. Murphy is the author of the Belltown Mystery Series and *Saving Santa's Seals*. Murphy has been featured in *101 Highly Successful Novelists*, and chosen by *Cape Cod Life Magazine* as One of the 400 People Who Brighten Our Lives. He spends his winters touring schools and his summers teaching young writers at The Writers' Shack in his hometown of Falmouth, Massachusetts. Visit www.Facebook.com/TheJustWriteItClass.

Mark Penta is a freelance illustrator and Hartford Art School graduate. His work has been published by Dell Magazines, Andrew McMeel, and featured on the Belltown Mystery book covers. He is the author/illustrator of several picture books, including *Cape Cod Invasion!* which was named a "Must-have product" by *Cape Cod Life Magazine*. He has taught drawing lessons to all ages, both privately and at schools like R.I.S.D. He also runs a fun and successful drawing service at private parties and corporate events. Visit www.MarkPenta.com

Learn more about their Totally Weird Activity Books at
www.TotallyWeirdActivityBooks.com and
www.facebook.com/TotallyWeirdActivityBooks

CPSIA information can be obtained
at www.ICGtesting.com
Printed in the USA
JSHW051707040423
39846JS00005BA/7